# Practical Guide to DOM

**Guide**

A. De Quattro

Copyright © 2024

Practical Guide

# 1.Introduction

The Document Object Model, commonly known as the DOM, is a fundamental concept in the field of web development. Understanding it is essential for any developer who wishes to programmatically manipulate the content, structure, and style of a web page. The DOM acts as a bridge between the HTML code that describes a web page and scripting languages, such as JavaScript, that interact with it. In this text, we will explore in detail the structure, functionality, and importance of the DOM, aiming to provide a comprehensive understanding of its workings and its role in modern web development.

### What is the DOM?

The DOM is an object representation of an HTML or XML document. It is essentially a structured map of the document that organizes elements into a hierarchical tree. Each node in this tree represents a part of the document, which can be an HTML element, an attribute, text, or a comment. This tree structure allows scripting languages like JavaScript to dynamically access and manipulate the contents of a web page.

### History and Development of the DOM

The concept of the DOM emerged in the late 1990s in response to the growing need to make web pages more dynamic and interactive. Before the advent of the DOM, web pages were static, and it was not possible to modify the content or structure of a page after it had been loaded into the browser. With the standardization of the DOM by the World Wide Web Consortium (W3C), developers gained a powerful tool for creating dynamic web applications.

The DOM was developed alongside the evolution of web browsers, and the early implementations varied significantly across different browsers, leading to compatibility issues. However, over time, the DOM evolved into a unified standard, supported by all major modern browsers, making cross-browser web application development easier.

### Structure of the DOM

The DOM represents an HTML document as a tree of objects. The root element of the tree is usually the `<html>` element, which contains other nodes like `<head>` and `<body>`. These nodes, in turn, can contain further elements such as `<div>`, `<p>`, `<a>`, and so on. Each element in the document is represented as a node in the DOM tree, and these nodes are connected to each other hierarchically.

#### Types of Nodes in the DOM

There are several types of nodes in the DOM, each playing a specific role in the document structure:

1. **Element Nodes:** Represent HTML elements (such as `<div>`, `<p>`, `<a>`, etc.). These are the most common nodes and make up the majority of the DOM tree.

2. **Text Nodes:** Represent the textual content within an HTML element. Any element containing text has a text node as its child.

3. **Attribute Nodes:** Represent attributes of an HTML element (such as `class`, `id`, `href`, etc.). In the DOM, attributes are generally considered properties of elements rather than standalone nodes, but in some versions of the DOM, they can be treated as nodes.

4. **Comment Nodes:** Represent comments inserted in the HTML code. Although comments are not visible on the web page, they are still part of the DOM and can be accessed via JavaScript.

5. **Document Nodes:** Represent the entire HTML document. The document node is the root of the DOM tree and serves as the starting point for accessing other nodes.

6. **DocumentFragment Nodes:** Are special nodes that act as temporary containers for groups of nodes. Document fragments are not part of the main document and are used for DOM manipulation operations that require optimized performance.

### Accessing and Manipulating the DOM

JavaScript is the primary language used to interact with the DOM. Through JavaScript, you can select elements, read and modify their content or attributes, create new elements and remove them, and even change the structure of the page.

#### Selecting Elements

To manipulate an element in the DOM, it must first be selected. JavaScript offers several methods to do this:

1. **`getElementById(id)`:** This method returns the element with the specified ID. It is one of the fastest ways to access a specific element since IDs are unique within a page.

```javascript
var element = document.getElementById('myID');
```

2. **`getElementsByClassName(className)`:** Returns a list (HTMLCollection) of all elements that have the specified class.

```javascript
var elements =
```

document.getElementsByClassName('myClass');
```

3. **`getElementsByTagName(tagName)`:** Returns a list of all elements with the specified tag name (e.g., `div`, `p`, `a`).

   ```javascript
   var paragraphs = document.getElementsByTagName('p');
   ```

4. **`querySelector(selector)`:** This method returns the first element that matches the specified CSS selector. It is very powerful and flexible, though it may be slightly slower than other selection methods.

   ```javascript
   var firstElement =

document.querySelector('.class .subClass');

```

5. **`querySelectorAll(selector)`:** Returns a NodeList of all elements that match the specified CSS selector.

```javascript
var allElements = document.querySelectorAll('.class .subClass');
```

#### Modifying Content

Once an element is selected, its content or attributes can be manipulated. Some of the most common methods include:

- **`innerHTML` and `textContent`:** These properties allow reading or setting the content
```

of an element. `innerHTML` also allows inserting HTML code within an element, while `textContent` inserts only plain text.

```javascript
// Set HTML content
element.innerHTML = "<strong>Bold text</strong>";

// Set plain text
element.textContent = "Plain text only";
```

- **`setAttribute(name, value)`:** This method allows setting an attribute on an element.

```javascript
element.setAttribute('class', 'newClass');
```

- **`style`:** The `style` property allows direct manipulation of an element's CSS styles.

```javascript
element.style.backgroundColor = "blue";
element.style.fontSize = "20px";
```

#### Creating and Removing Elements

The DOM also allows the creation of new elements or the removal of existing ones.

- **`createElement(tagName)`:** This method creates a new element of the specified type.

```javascript
var newDiv =
```

```javascript
document.createElement('div');
newDiv.textContent = "I am a new div!";
```

- **`appendChild(node)`:** Adds a node as a child of the selected element.

```javascript
document.body.appendChild(newDiv);
```

- **`removeChild(node)`:** Removes a child node from the selected element.

```javascript
var elementToRemove = document.getElementById('oldID');

elementToRemove.parentNode.removeChild(elementToRemove);
```

```

- **`replaceChild(newNode, oldNode)`:** Replaces a child node with another node.

```javascript
var newElement = document.createElement('p');
newElement.textContent = "New paragraph!";
var oldElement = document.getElementById('oldID');
oldElement.parentNode.replaceChild(newElement, oldElement);
```

#### DOM Events

The DOM is not just a static structure; it also
```

supports dynamic interaction through events. Events are actions or occurrences that happen in the document and can be intercepted to execute specific code. Common events include mouse clicks, key presses, page loads, and more.

- **Mouse Events:** Such as `click`, `dblclick`, `mouseover`, `mouseout`.

```javascript
element.addEventListener('click', function() {
    alert('Element clicked!');
});
```

- **Keyboard Events:** Such as `keydown`, `keyup`, `keypress`.

```javascript
```

```javascript
document.addEventListener('keydown', function(event) {
    console.log('Key pressed: ' + event.key);
});
```

- **Window Events:** Such as `load`, `resize`, `scroll`.

```javascript
window.addEventListener('resize', function() {
    console.log('The window has been resized.');
});
```

Events can be attached to elements using the `addEventListener` method, which allows specifying the type of event to listen for and the function to execute when the event occurs.

### Practical Examples of DOM Manipulation

To better understand how the DOM works, let's consider a practical example. Suppose we want to create a dynamic list of items that the user can add or remove.

```html
<!DOCTYPE html>
<html lang="en">
<head>
    <meta charset="UTF-8">
    <meta name="viewport" content="width=device-width, initial-scale=1.0">
    <title>DOM Example</title>
</head>
```

```html
<body>
    <h1>Dynamic List</h1>
    <ul id="list"></ul>
    <input type="text" id="newItem" placeholder="New item">
    <button id="add">Add</button>
    <script>
        var list = document.getElementById('list');
        var input = document.getElementById('newItem');
        var add = document.getElementById('add');

        add.addEventListener('click', function() {
            var text = input.value;
            if (text !== "") {
                var newItem = document.createElement('li');
                newItem.textContent = text;
```

```
        var removeButton = document.createElement('button');
        removeButton.textContent = "Remove";

removeButton.addEventListener('click', function() {
                list.removeChild(newItem);
        });


newItem.appendChild(removeButton);
        list.appendChild(newItem);

        input.value = "";
    }
  });
```

```
    </script>
</body>
</html>
```

In this example, we create a simple web page where users can add items to a list and remove them. We use the `createElement`, `appendChild`, and `removeChild` methods to dynamically manipulate the DOM and manage the list items. This demonstrates how powerful and flexible the DOM is for creating interactive web applications.

### Conclusion

The Document Object Model is a key technology in web development, enabling developers to create dynamic and interactive websites. By mastering the DOM, you can access and manipulate the structure and content of web pages programmatically, creating a more engaging and responsive user experience. The DOM provides a standardized way to interact with web documents, making it a crucial tool in modern web development.

### 2. Theoretical Foundations of the W3C Document Object Model (DOM)

Through the DOM, programmers can interact with the structure of a document in a programmable way, manipulating and accessing the elements and attributes that compose it. This comprehensive text delves into the theoretical foundations of the W3C DOM, exploring key definitions, the history and development of the model, as well as the basic principles that form its foundation.

### Key Definitions

Before diving into the history and principles of the DOM, it's crucial to understand some key definitions that form the theoretical basis of this model.

#### 1. Document Object Model (DOM)

The DOM is a programming interface for HTML and XML documents. It represents the structure of a document as a tree of nodes, where each node corresponds to a part of the document, such as an element, attribute, or piece of text. This tree representation allows scripting languages, like JavaScript, to interact with the document by modifying its content, structure, and style.

#### 2. Node

A node is a fundamental unit of the DOM. Every part of an HTML or XML document is represented as a node in the DOM, which can be of various types, such as an element, text, attribute, comment, or the document itself. Nodes are connected in a tree structure, where a node can have zero or more child nodes.

#### 3. DOM Tree

The DOM tree is the hierarchical structure that represents a document in a way that is easily navigable and manipulable. The root element of the tree is typically the `<html>` element in an HTML document. From this root node, all other nodes branch out, forming a structure that represents the entire document.

#### 4. Attribute

In the context of the DOM, an attribute is a special type of node associated with an HTML or XML element. Attributes provide additional information about elements and can be programmatically manipulated. For example, the `class` attribute in an HTML element can be modified to change the element's behavior or style.

#### 5. Application Programming Interface (API)

The DOM is essentially an API, a set of functions and methods that programmers can use to interact with the document. Through the DOM API, it's possible to select, create, modify, and delete nodes, as well as respond to events such as mouse clicks or keyboard input.

#### 6. Document

The term "document" in the context of the DOM refers to any HTML or XML file that is interpreted and represented as a DOM tree. The document is the root of the DOM tree and serves as the starting point for interacting with all other nodes.

### History and Development

The DOM did not appear overnight but is the result of a long process of evolution and standardization involving various actors and technologies over the years. Below, we analyze the history and development of the DOM, from its inception to its current standardized form.

#### 1. Origins of the DOM

The early versions of web browsers, like Mosaic and Netscape Navigator, were designed to display static HTML documents. These browsers did not allow dynamic manipulation of page content once it was loaded. However, with the increasing complexity of web applications and the growing demand for interactive pages, a solution was needed that would allow programmers to modify the content and structure of web pages dynamically.

In the mid-1990s, the need for interactivity and dynamism on the web led to the introduction of technologies like JavaScript, which allowed code to be executed directly in the browser. However, in these early stages, each browser had its own model for interacting with the document, leading to fragmentation and compatibility issues.

## 2. Introduction of DOM

"DOM Level 0" was not truly a standard but rather a series of unofficial and inconsistent methods implemented by early browsers to allow some level of interactivity in web pages. These methods enabled access to and modification of certain document elements, such as the page title (`document.title`) or forms (`document.forms`).

However, the lack of consistency between different browsers made it difficult for programmers to write code that worked across multiple platforms. This led to the need for standardization.

#### 3. Standardization and DOM Level 1

In 1998, the World Wide Web Consortium (W3C) introduced DOM Level 1, the first attempt to create a standardized interface for accessing and manipulating HTML and XML documents. This standard clearly defined how browsers should represent documents as a tree of nodes and which methods and properties should be available to interact with these nodes.

DOM Level 1 laid the groundwork for navigating and manipulating the DOM tree, allowing programmers to access elements, modify attributes, create new nodes, and delete existing ones. This standard made it possible to develop more complex and interactive web pages, providing a common base that various browsers could implement.

#### 4. Evolution of the DOM: Levels 2 and 3

With DOM Level 2, introduced in 2000, new functionalities were added, such as support for events, styles, and namespaces. These extensions allowed programmers to write more sophisticated code, responding to user events (like clicks or mouse movements) and directly manipulating CSS styles through the

DOM.

DOM Level 3, introduced in 2004, further expanded the DOM's capabilities, adding support for querying XML documents, handling exceptions, and improving support for namespaces and XML document manipulation.

With these subsequent versions, the DOM became a powerful and flexible tool, used not only for managing HTML documents but also for other XML applications, such as SVG (Scalable Vector Graphics) and MathML (Mathematical Markup Language).

#### 5. HTML5 DOM and Modern Adoption

With the introduction of HTML5, the DOM underwent further improvements to align with the new features of the language. HTML5 integrated many of the DOM functionalities that previously required complex scripts or external plugins, making it easier for developers to create rich and interactive web pages.

Moreover, modern browsers have continued to evolve to fully support the DOM, improving performance and interoperability. Today, the DOM is a universally accepted and supported standard, used in virtually all modern web applications.

### Basic Principles of the DOM

The DOM is based on a series of fundamental principles that define its behavior and structure. These principles ensure that the DOM is consistent, predictable, and effectively usable by developers. Below, we explore some of the most important basic principles.

#### 1. Tree Hierarchy

One of the most fundamental principles of the

DOM is that it represents a document as a tree hierarchy. In this tree structure, each node represents a part of the document, and nodes are organized hierarchically. The root node, which is often the `<html>` element in an HTML document, is the starting point for the entire tree. From here, various branches extend, representing nested elements such as `<head>`, `<body>`, and all their children.

This tree hierarchy allows for easy navigation of the document and manipulation of individual elements or entire branches of the document. For example, if you want to access a particular paragraph within a `<div>`, you can traverse the tree starting from the root node until you find the desired element.

#### 2. Node Types

The DOM defines several types of nodes, each with a specific role in representing the document's structure. The most common node types include:

- **Element Nodes:** Represent HTML or XML elements. Each element node can have attributes, text, and children.

- **Text Nodes:** Contain the text within an element. A text node cannot have children or attributes; it is a leaf node in the DOM tree.

- **Attribute Nodes:** Represent the attributes of an element. Although associated with an element node, attributes are not children of the element node in the DOM.

- **Comment Nodes:** Represent comments within the document.

These node types allow the DOM to faithfully represent every part of a document, from the structure of elements to the text content and attributes of elements.

#### 3. Access and Navigation

A key principle of the DOM is the ability to easily access and navigate through the document's tree structure. The DOM provides various properties and methods for this purpose, including:

- **`parentNode`:** Returns the parent node of a node.

- **`childNodes`:** Returns a collection of all child nodes of a node.

- **`firstChild` and `lastChild`:** Return the first and last child nodes, respectively.

- **`nextSibling` and `previousSibling`:** Allow navigation between sibling nodes.

These properties and methods enable

exploration of the entire DOM tree, accessing any node and manipulating its content or structure.

#### 4. Dynamism

One of the main advantages of the DOM is its dynamism. Developers can create new nodes, modify existing nodes, or delete nodes from the document, all in real-time. This dynamism is what allows the creation of interactive and responsive web pages.

For example, methods like `createElement`, `appendChild`, `removeChild`, and `setAttribute` can be used to directly manipulate the document structure, adding or removing elements or modifying their attributes.

#### 5. Event Handling

The DOM is not just a static representation of a document's structure; it also includes a powerful event-handling system. Events are actions or occurrences, such as a mouse click, a keypress, or a page load, that can be handled by JavaScript code.

The DOM allows attaching event listeners to specific nodes in the tree, enabling dynamic responses to these events. For example, you can use `addEventListener` to attach a function to a specific event, like a button click:

```javascript
button.addEventListener('click', function() {
    alert('Button clicked!');
});
```

#### 6. Language Independence

The DOM is designed to be independent of the programming language used. Although JavaScript is the language most commonly associated with the DOM, the DOM structure can be manipulated by any scripting or programming language that supports the DOM interface. This makes the DOM a versatile and universal model, usable in different contexts and platforms.

The Document Object Model (DOM) is an essential

concept for understanding modern web development. By providing a programmable interface for accessing and manipulating documents, the DOM enables the creation of dynamic, interactive, and responsive web applications. Understanding its theoretical foundations—such as its history, key definitions, and basic principles—allows developers to harness the full power of the DOM and create more efficient and effective web applications.

# 3. DOM Approaches and Techniques

The Document Object Model (DOM) is one of the fundamental technologies for the modern web, essential for dynamic interaction with web pages. Exploring various approaches and techniques for working with the DOM is crucial for understanding how to efficiently manipulate HTML and XML documents. In this guide, we will delve into data collection methodologies and result analysis through the DOM, how to detect the DOM, and discuss the use of the `document` object, elements, and nodes, with practical examples illustrating each concept.

### Data Collection via the DOM

Data collection via the DOM refers to the acquisition of structured information from an HTML or XML document. This process can be used to analyze content, extract useful information, or monitor user interactions.

#### 1. Element Selection

To collect data from the DOM, it is essential to know how to select the appropriate elements. There are several methods to do this:

- **`getElementById(id)`:** Selects a specific element based on its `id` attribute.

```javascript
var title = document.getElementById('title');
console.log(title.textContent);
```

- **`getElementsByClassName(className)`:** Selects all elements with a specific class.

```javascript
var articles = document.getElementsByClassName('article');
for (var i = 0; i < articles.length; i++) {
    console.log(articles[i].textContent);
}
```

- **`getElementsByTagName(tagName)`:** Selects all elements with a specific tag name.

```javascript
var paragraphs = document.getElementsByTagName('p');
for (var i = 0; i < paragraphs.length; i++) {
    console.log(paragraphs[i].textContent);
}
```

- **`querySelector(selector)`:** Selects the first element that matches a CSS selector.

```javascript
var firstParagraph = document.querySelector('p');
console.log(firstParagraph.textContent);
```

- **`querySelectorAll(selector)`:** Selects all elements that match a CSS selector.

```javascript
var allParagraphs = document.querySelectorAll('p');
allParagraphs.forEach(function(paragraph) {
    console.log(paragraph.textContent);
});
```

#### 2. Extracting Data from Elements

Once the desired elements are selected, data can be extracted using various DOM properties and methods:

- **`textContent`:** Returns or sets the text content of an element, including its descendants.

    ```javascript
    var titleText = title.textContent;
    console.log(titleText);
    ```

- **`innerHTML`:** Returns or sets the HTML content inside an element.

    ```javascript
    var htmlContent =
    ```

```javascript
document.getElementById('content').innerHTML;
console.log(htmlContent);
```

- **`value`:** Used to get or set the value of an input, selection, textarea, etc.

```javascript
var inputValue = document.getElementById('username').value;
console.log(inputValue);
```

- **`getAttribute(attrName)`:** Returns the value of a specific attribute of an element.

```javascript
var href = document.querySelector('a').getAttribute('href'
```

);

```
console.log(href);
```

#### 3. Collecting Data from Forms

One of the most common uses of data collection is gathering information from users through forms. User-entered data can be collected and subsequently processed or sent to a server.

```html
<form id="contactForm">
    <input type="text" id="name" name="name" placeholder="Name">
    <input type="email" id="email" name="email" placeholder="Email">
    <textarea id="message" name="message" placeholder="Message"></textarea>
```

```html
    <button type="submit">Send</button>
</form>


<script>

document.getElementById('contactForm').addEventListener('submit', function(event) {

    event.preventDefault();

    var name = document.getElementById('name').value;

    var email = document.getElementById('email').value;

    var message = document.getElementById('message').value;


    console.log('Name:', name);

    console.log('Email:', email);

    console.log('Message:', message);

});
</script>
```

```

In this example, form data is collected when the user presses the submit button. The `submit` event is intercepted, the data is gathered, and printed to the console.

### Result Analysis

Analyzing the results obtained through DOM data collection is crucial for understanding user behavior or the state of the web page. Once data is collected, it can be processed, analyzed, and used to make decisions or generate output.

#### 1. Basic Analysis

After data collection, the next step is to analyze it. This can involve checking certain conditions, comparing values, or displaying the data in a useful format.
```

```javascript
var paragraphs = document.querySelectorAll('p');
paragraphs.forEach(function(paragraph, index) {
    console.log('Paragraph ' + (index + 1) + ': ' + paragraph.textContent);
});
```

In this example, all paragraphs are listed with their content, providing a simple analysis of the text present on the page.

#### 2. Conditions and Filters

Conditions and filters can be applied to better analyze collected data. For example, if you want to find all elements containing a specific keyword:

```javascript
var keyword = "important";
var importantParagraphs = [];

document.querySelectorAll('p').forEach(function(paragraph) {
    if (paragraph.textContent.includes(keyword)) {
        importantParagraphs.push(paragraph);
    }
});

console.log('Important paragraphs:', importantParagraphs);
```

This code collects all paragraphs containing the word "important" and saves them in an array for further analysis.

#### 3. Data Aggregation

In some cases, it is useful to aggregate data to obtain summary information. For example, you may want to calculate the sum of all numeric values in a list:

```javascript
var values = document.querySelectorAll('.value');
var sum = 0;

values.forEach(function(value) {
    sum += parseFloat(value.textContent);
});

console.log('Total sum:', sum);
```

In this example, all numeric values within elements with the `value` class are summed to obtain an overall total.

### Detecting the DOM

Detecting the DOM refers to knowing when the DOM is fully loaded and ready for interaction. This phase is crucial to ensure that manipulations and scripts are executed at the right time.

#### 1. `DOMContentLoaded` Event

The `DOMContentLoaded` event is triggered when the HTML document has been completely loaded and parsed, without waiting for styles, images, or subresources to load.

```javascript
document.addEventListener('DOMContentLoaded', function() {
```

```javascript
    console.log('The DOM is fully loaded and ready.');
});
```

This event is useful when you want to execute a script as soon as the DOM is ready, but without waiting for the entire page to load.

#### 2. `load` Event

The `load` event is triggered when the entire page, including resources like images and CSS styles, has fully loaded.

```javascript
window.addEventListener('load', function() {
    console.log('The page is fully loaded.');
});
```

Using the `load` event is appropriate when it is necessary to ensure that all external resources have loaded before executing the code.

#### 3. Differences between `DOMContentLoaded` and `load`

The choice between `DOMContentLoaded` and `load` depends on the application's needs. If interaction with the DOM is independent of resource loading, `DOMContentLoaded` is generally faster. However, if the code depends on images or other external content, the `load` event ensures that everything is available.

### The `document` Object

The `document` object is the root of the DOM. It contains all the information and methods needed to interact with the loaded HTML or XML document.

#### 1. Key Properties

The `document` object has numerous useful properties:

- **`document.title`:** Returns or sets the document's title.

    ```javascript
    console.log(document.title);
    document.title = "New Page Title";
    ```

- **`document.URL`:** Returns the full URL of the document.

    ```javascript
    console.log(document.URL);
    ```

- **`document.body`:** Returns the document's `<body>` element.

    ```javascript
    console.log(document.body);
    ```

- **`document.head`:** Returns the document's `<head>` element.

    ```javascript
    console.log(document.head);
    ```

- **`document.forms`:** Returns a collection of all the forms in the document.

    ```javascript
    ```

```javascript
var forms = document.forms;
for (var i = 0; i < forms.length; i++) {
  console.log(forms[i].name);
}
```

#### 2. Key Methods

The `document` object offers numerous methods for manipulating the document's content:

- **`createElement(tagName)`:** Creates a new HTML element with the specified tag name.

```javascript
var newParagraph = document.createElement('p');
newParagraph.textContent = "This is a new
```

paragraph.";

document.body.appendChild(newParagraph);
```

- **`createTextNode(data)`:** Creates a new text node with the specified content.

```javascript
var text = document.createTextNode("This is simple text.");
document.body.appendChild(text);
```

- **`getElementById(id)`:** Selects an element with a specific ID.

```javascript
var element = document.get

ElementById('myElement');
console.log(element);
```

- **`getElementsByClassName(className)`:** Selects all elements with a specific class name.

```javascript
var elements = document.getElementsByClassName('myClass');
console.log(elements.length);
```

- **`getElementsByTagName(tagName)`:** Selects all elements with a specific tag name.

```javascript

```javascript
var elements = document.getElementsByTagName('p');
console.log(elements.length);
```

### Elements and Nodes

Understanding the difference between elements and nodes is fundamental to DOM manipulation.

#### 1. Elements

Elements represent the HTML tags in the document. They can be manipulated directly using the properties and methods discussed above.

```javascript
var header =
```

```
document.querySelector('header');

header.style.backgroundColor = "blue";
```

#### 2. Nodes

Nodes are more general and include elements, text nodes, comments, and other parts of the document. The DOM treats the entire document as a tree of nodes.

```javascript
var firstChild = document.body.firstChild;

console.log(firstChild.nodeName);
```

Working with the DOM involves selecting elements, collecting data, analyzing results, and knowing when the DOM is ready for interaction. The `document` object provides the necessary tools to manipulate the DOM effectively, while understanding the differences between elements and nodes helps in navigating the document's structure. Whether you are building interactive features, gathering user input, or analyzing web content, mastering DOM approaches and techniques is essential for any web developer.

## 4. The DOM in Browsers

The Document Object Model (DOM) is an essential part of modern web architecture. It serves as the programmatic interface that allows scripting languages like JavaScript to dynamically interact with the content of an HTML or XML document. However, the DOM is not a universal abstract technology; it is implemented specifically in each web browser, with slight differences that can affect the behavior of complex scripts.

In this detailed guide, we will examine how the DOM is implemented in major browsers, exploring the peculiarities of each implementation and providing practical examples. We will then delve into how to extend the DOM with JavaScript, creating new methods and properties to customize and enhance interaction with web documents.

### DOM Implementation in Browsers

Each browser implements the DOM slightly differently, as the DOM is a specification that browser vendors must follow. Although modern browsers have made significant strides toward standards compliance, important differences still exist that are useful to know.

#### 1. Chrome (Blink-Based)

Google Chrome uses Blink as its rendering engine, a fork of WebKit. Blink is widely considered one of the fastest and most standards-compliant DOM engines, with frequent updates to support the latest web features.

**Example:** Selecting and manipulating elements in Chrome.

```javascript
// Selecting an element by ID
```

```javascript
var element = document.getElementById('myElement');

// Changing the element's style
element.style.color = 'blue';

// Adding a new text node
var newText = document.createTextNode('New text');
element.appendChild(newText);
```

In Chrome, these operations are performed very smoothly thanks to Blink's optimization for DOM manipulation.

#### 2. Firefox (Gecko-Based)

Firefox uses Gecko, an open-source rendering engine developed by Mozilla. Gecko is known for its focus on standards compliance and user privacy, as well as being a robust environment for testing DOM behavior.

**Example:** Navigating between nodes in Firefox.

```javascript
// Selecting the parent node
var parent = element.parentNode;

// Selecting the first child node
var firstChild = parent.firstChild;

// Modifying the content of the first child
firstChild.textContent = 'Modified content';
```

Firefox handles these operations reliably, with

solid support for advanced DOM features.

#### 3. Safari (WebKit-Based)

Safari, the default browser on Apple devices, uses WebKit as its rendering engine. WebKit is known for its energy efficiency on mobile devices and its compatibility with standard web technologies.

**Example:** Manipulating attributes in Safari.

```javascript
// Adding an attribute to an element

element.setAttribute('data-custom', 'customValue');

// Retrieving the attribute

var attrValue = element.getAttribute('data-
```

custom');

// Changing the attribute's value

element.setAttribute('data-custom', 'newValue');
```

Safari handles these operations well, though there may be slight rendering differences compared to other browsers, especially on iOS.

#### 4. Microsoft Edge (Blink-Based)

Microsoft Edge, originally based on EdgeHTML, now uses Blink, the same engine as Chrome. This has led Edge to behave very similarly to Chrome, with few differences.

**Example:** Dynamically adding elements in Edge.
```

```javascript
// Creating a new div element
var newDiv = document.createElement('div');

// Setting attributes and content
newDiv.id = 'newDiv';
newDiv.textContent = 'This is a new div.';

// Adding the div to the body
document.body.appendChild(newDiv);
```

Thanks to the adoption of Blink, Edge has significantly improved its speed and compatibility with the latest DOM technologies.

#### 5. Opera (Blink-Based)

Opera, like Chrome and Edge, uses Blink. Opera offers unique features such as a built-in VPN, but its DOM handling is essentially the same as Chrome's.

**Example:** Animating elements in Opera.

```javascript
// Changing an element's position
element.style.position = 'absolute';
element.style.left = '0px';

// Animating the position
function moveElement() {
   var position = parseInt(element.style.left, 10);
   if (position < 200) {
      element.style.left = (position + 1) + 'px';
      requestAnimationFrame(moveElement);
```

```
    }
}
moveElement();
```

Opera performs this type of animation with the same efficiency as Chrome, thanks to using the Blink engine.

### Extending the DOM with JavaScript

Extending the DOM with JavaScript is a powerful technique for customizing and enhancing web page functionality. It allows you to add new methods and properties to existing DOM objects or create new types of elements and behaviors.

#### 1. Adding Custom Methods to Elements

You can extend DOM elements by adding new methods to their prototypes. This allows you to create reusable functionality that can be applied to any element.

**Example:** Adding a custom method to all `div` elements.

```javascript
// Adding a method to the HTMLDivElement prototype
HTMLDivElement.prototype.colorRed = function() {
    this.style.backgroundColor = 'red';
};

// Using the new method on a div
var myDiv = document.getElementById('myDiv');
myDiv.colorRed();
```

```

This example shows how to extend all `div` elements by adding a `colorRed` method that changes the `div`'s background to red.

#### 2. Creating Custom DOM Objects

In some cases, it may be useful to create new types of DOM elements with custom behaviors. This can be done by creating JavaScript classes that extend existing DOM elements.

**Example:** Creating a new type of `SuperDiv` element.

```javascript
// Creating a class that extends HTMLDivElement

class SuperDiv extends HTMLDivElement {

```
  constructor() {
    super();
    this.style.border = '2px solid black';
    this.textContent = 'I am a SuperDiv!';
  }

  highlight() {
    this.style.backgroundColor = 'yellow';
  }
}

// Defining the new custom element
customElements.define('super-div', SuperDiv, { extends: 'div' });

// Using the new element
var superDiv = new SuperDiv();
document.body.appendChild(superDiv);
```

```
// Calling the custom method
superDiv.highlight();
```

In this example, we've created a new type of `div` called `SuperDiv` with unique behavior. This type of element can be used anywhere on the page, extending the standard DOM functionality.

#### 3. Modifying Existing DOM Behavior

It is also possible to modify the behavior of existing DOM elements by overriding their prototype methods.

**Example:** Overriding the `appendChild` method.

```javascript
```

```javascript
// Saving a copy of the original method
var oldAppendChild = Node.prototype.appendChild;


// Overriding appendChild
Node.prototype.appendChild = function(childNode) {
    console.log('Adding a node:', childNode);
    // Calling the original method
    return oldAppendChild.call(this, childNode);
};


// Testing the new behavior
var newElement = document.createElement('p');
newElement.textContent = 'Dynamically added text.';
document.body.appendChild(newElement);
```

Here we've overridden the `appendChild` method to log every time a new node is added to the DOM while preserving the original behavior.

#### 4. Creating Custom Elements (Web Components)

Web Components are a set of APIs that allow you to create custom elements that can be reused anywhere on a website. These elements can have their own markup, style, and behavior.

**Example:** Creating a Custom Element.

```javascript
// Defining a new element called my-element
class MyElement extends HTMLElement {
    constructor() {
        super();
```

```javascript
    // Creating a shadow DOM for the element
    var shadow = this.attachShadow({ mode: 'open' });

    // Creating a paragraph inside the shadow DOM
    var paragraph = document.createElement('p');
    paragraph.textContent = 'Hello, I am a Web Component!';

    // Attaching the paragraph to the shadow DOM
    shadow.appendChild(paragraph);
  }
}

// Defining the new custom element
customElements.define('my-element',
```

```
MyElement);


// Using the new element in the DOM
var newElement = document.createElement('my-element');
document.body.appendChild(newElement);
```

This example illustrates how to create a simple Web Component that can be reused like any other HTML element.

The Document Object Model (DOM) is a central aspect of web development, and each browser implements it with its specific nuances. Understanding these differences is crucial for developing web applications that work smoothly across different platforms. Additionally, the ability to extend the DOM with JavaScript allows for highly customized solutions, enhancing interactivity and user experience.

Through the use of prototypes, custom classes, and Web Components, it is possible to transform how we interact with the DOM, taking web development to a higher level. The techniques explored in this guide are just the beginning of what can be achieved with the DOM and JavaScript. With creativity and a deep understanding, the possibilities are virtually endless.

# 5. Examples and Applications of the DOM

The Document Object Model (DOM) is key to dynamically interacting with and manipulating HTML and XML documents within browsers. Understanding how to manage attributes, retrieve elements, manipulate document structure, and use properties like `innerHTML` is essential for building interactive and responsive web applications.

In this guide, we will explore these concepts with practical examples, offering a step-by-step tutorial and concluding with a collection of useful resources for further study.

### Managing Attributes in the DOM

Attributes are specific properties of HTML elements that provide additional information or configure the behavior of an element. In the DOM, attributes can be read, modified, added, or removed using dedicated methods.

#### 1. Retrieving Attributes

To retrieve the value of an element's attribute, use the `getAttribute(attrName)` method.

**Example:**

```javascript
// Select an element by its ID
var element = document.getElementById('link');

// Retrieve the value of the href attribute
var hrefValue = element.getAttribute('href');
console.log(hrefValue);  // Output: The URL of the link
```

In this example, we retrieve the value of the

`href` attribute of a link to know which URL it points to.

#### 2. Setting and Modifying Attributes

To set or modify an attribute, use the `setAttribute(attrName, value)` method.

**Example:**

```javascript
// Modify the href attribute of the link
element.setAttribute('href', 'https://www.new-url.com');
```

In this case, the link's URL is updated to a new value.

#### 3. Removing Attributes

Attributes can also be removed using `removeAttribute(attrName)`.

**Example:**

```javascript
// Remove the target attribute from the link
element.removeAttribute('target');
```

Removing the `target` attribute will disable the link from opening in a new window or tab.

### Retrieving Elements from the DOM

Retrieving specific elements from the DOM is fundamental for any manipulation operation. There are various methods to select elements, each suitable for different scenarios.

#### 1. `getElementById`

This method is used to select a single element by its `id`, which should be unique in the document.

**Example:**

```javascript
var header = document.getElementById('main-header');
console.log(header.textContent); // Output: The text of the main header
```

#### 2. `getElementsByClassName`

This method returns a collection of all elements that have a certain class.

**Example:**

```javascript
var elementsWithClass = document.getElementsByClassName('highlight');

for (var i = 0; i < elementsWithClass.length; i++) {

console.log(elementsWithClass[i].textContent);
}
```

This example retrieves all elements with the class `highlight` and prints their text content.

#### 3. `getElementsByTagName`

This method selects all elements with a given tag name.

**Example:**

```javascript
var paragraphs = document.getElementsByTagName('p');
console.log('Number of paragraphs:', paragraphs.length);
```

Here, we are counting how many `<p>` elements are present in the document.

#### 4. `querySelector` and `querySelectorAll`

`querySelector` selects the first element that matches a specified CSS selector, while `querySelectorAll` returns all elements that match the selector.

**Example:**

```javascript
// Select the first element with the class 'intro'
var intro = document.querySelector('.intro');
console.log(intro.textContent);

// Select all elements with the class 'item'
var items = document.querySelectorAll('.item');
items.forEach(function(item) {
   console.log(item.textContent);
});
```

These methods are very flexible and powerful, especially when using complex selectors.

### Manipulating the Document Structure

Manipulating the document structure means adding, removing, or modifying elements within the DOM. These operations are crucial for creating dynamic interfaces.

#### 1. Adding Elements

Elements can be dynamically created and added to the DOM using `createElement` and `appendChild`.

**Example:**

```javascript
// Create a new <div> element
var newDiv = document.createElement('div');

// Set an ID and content for the new div
newDiv.id = 'newDiv';
newDiv.textContent = 'This is a new div
```

created dynamically.';

// Add the new div to the document body

document.body.appendChild(newDiv);
```

This code creates a new `div` element and adds it to the end of the document body.

#### 2. Removing Elements

Elements can be removed from the DOM using `removeChild`.

**Example:**

```javascript
// Select the element to be removed

var elementToRemove =

```javascript
document.getElementById('elementID');

// Remove the element from its parent
elementToRemove.parentNode.removeChild(elementToRemove);
```

This example shows how to remove a specific element from the DOM structure.

#### 3. Replacing Elements

Elements can be replaced using `replaceChild`.

**Example:**

```javascript
// Create a new paragraph element
```

```
var newParagraph = document.createElement('p');

newParagraph.textContent = 'This is a replacement paragraph.';


// Select the element to be replaced

var oldElement = document.getElementById('oldElement');


// Replace the old element with the new paragraph

oldElement.parentNode.replaceChild(newParagraph, oldElement);
```

This code replaces an existing element with a new paragraph.


### Using `innerHTML` to Manipulate Content

The `innerHTML` property allows you to read or write the HTML content of an element. It is a powerful tool for quickly updating parts of the DOM but requires caution to avoid security risks like Cross-Site Scripting (XSS) attacks.

#### 1. Reading HTML Content

**Example:**

```javascript
// Select an element and read its HTML content
var divContent = document.getElementById('content').innerHTML;
console.log(divContent);
```

This code reads the HTML content of an

element and prints it to the console.

#### 2. Writing or Updating HTML Content

**Example:**

```javascript
// Update the HTML content of an element
document.getElementById('content').innerHTML = '<p>New HTML content added dynamically.</p>';
```

Here, we are replacing the HTML content of an element with a new paragraph.

#### 3. Adding Content Safely

To prevent security issues, you can construct

the DOM using methods like `createElement` and `appendChild` instead of `innerHTML` when incorporating content from untrusted sources.

**Example:**

```javascript
// Create a new anchor element
var safeLink = document.createElement('a');
safeLink.textContent = 'Click here';
safeLink.href = 'https://www.example.com';

// Add the link safely
document.getElementById('content').appendChild(safeLink);
```

This example adds a link safely, avoiding the direct use of `innerHTML`.

### Final Tutorial: Creating a Dynamic Interface

To consolidate what we've learned, we'll create a simple dynamic interface that allows the user to add, modify, and remove items from a list.

**Complete Example:**

```html
<!DOCTYPE html>
<html lang="en">
<head>
    <meta charset="UTF-8">
    <meta name="viewport" content="width=device-width, initial-scale=1.0">
    <title>List Management</title>
    <style>
```

```css
#list {
    margin: 20px 0;
    padding: 0;
    list-style-type: none;
}
#list li {
    padding: 8px;
    border: 1px solid #ccc;
    margin-bottom: 5px;
}
```
```html
    </style>
</head>
<body>

    <h1>List Management</h1>

    <input type="text" id="newItem" placeholder="Add a new item">
```

```html
<button id="addBtn">Add</button>

<ul id="list">
  <li>Item 1</li>
  <li>Item 2</li>
</ul>

<script>
  // Select the elements
  var list = document.getElementById('list');
  var input = document.getElementById('newItem');
  var addBtn = document.getElementById('addBtn');

  // Function to add a new item to the list
  function addItem() {
    var newText = input.value;
```

```javascript
        if (newText.trim() !== '') {
            var newLi = document.createElement('li');
            newLi.textContent = newText;

            // Add a remove button
            var removeBtn = document.createElement('button');
            removeBtn.textContent = 'Remove';
            removeBtn.style.marginLeft = '10px';
            removeBtn.onclick = function() {
                list.removeChild(newLi);
            };

            newLi.appendChild(removeBtn);
            list.appendChild(newLi);
            input.value = '';
        }
```

```
    }


    // Add click event to the add button
    addBtn.onclick = addItem;


    // Add item by pressing Enter
    input.addEventListener('keypress', function(event) {
        if (event.key === 'Enter') {
            addItem();
        }
    });
  </script>

</body>
</html>
```

This example creates an interface where the user can add new items to a list, with the option to remove them. Each time a new item is added, a "Remove" button is also generated to manage the item's removal.

The DOM is a crucial technology for modern web development, enabling the creation of dynamic and responsive user interfaces. By managing attributes, selecting and manipulating elements, and using properties like `innerHTML`, you can build feature-rich web applications. With the techniques and examples provided in this guide

, you should have a solid foundation to make the most of the DOM in your future projects.

## 6. DOM Glossary: Definitions and Key Concepts

The Document Object Model (DOM) is a programming interface that represents the structure of an HTML or XML document so that scripting languages like JavaScript can interact with it. To effectively understand and use the DOM, it's helpful to familiarize yourself with a range of key terms and concepts. This glossary provides detailed definitions of the main terms and concepts associated with the DOM.

#### 1. **Document Object Model (DOM)**

The Document Object Model (DOM) is an in-memory representation of a web document. It is a programming interface that allows scripting languages, such as JavaScript, to modify the structure, content, and style of an HTML or XML document. The DOM represents the document as a hierarchy of nodes, where each node is an object that can be manipulated through scripts.

#### 2. **Document**

The document is the primary object in the DOM. In an HTML document, the document represents the entire HTML file loaded in the browser. In an XML document, it represents the content of the XML. The document is the root node of the DOM structure and provides access to all other nodes through the `document` interface.

#### 3. **Node**

A node is a single unit within the DOM structure. Every element in the DOM is represented by a node. Nodes can be of different types, including:

- **Element Nodes**: Represent HTML or XML elements, such as `<div>`, `<p>`, `<a>`, etc.

- **Text Nodes**: Contain the text inside an element, such as the content between `<p>...</p>` tags.

- **Attribute Nodes**: Represent the attributes of elements, such as `id`, `class`, etc. (though in many modern DOM environments, attribute nodes are handled as part of element nodes).

- **Comment Nodes**: Contain comments in the document, such as `<!-- This is a comment -->`.

- **Document Nodes**: Represent the entire HTML or XML document.

#### 4. **Element**

An element is a type of node that represents a component of the document. HTML elements are defined by HTML tags, such as `<div>`, `<span>`, and `<ul>`. XML elements are defined by XML tags. Elements can have attributes and can contain other elements or text.

#### 5. **Attribute**

Attributes provide additional information about elements. Each attribute has a name and a value and is defined within the opening tags of elements. For example, in `<a href="https://www.example.com">`, `href` is an attribute of the `<a>` element, and `https://www.example.com` is its value.

#### 6. **Root Node**

The root node is the first node of the DOM structure and represents the entire document. In an HTML document, the root node is the `<html>` element. All other nodes are descendants of this root node.

#### 7. **Child Node**

A child node is a node that is directly contained within another node. For example, in `<div><p>Text</p></div>`, the `<p>` node is a child node of the `<div>` node, and the text node "Text" is a child node of the `<p>` node.

#### 8. **Parent Node**

A parent node is a node that contains one or more child nodes. For example, in `<div><p>Text</p></div>`, the `<div>` node is the parent node of the `<p>` node.

#### 9. **Sibling Node**

Sibling nodes are nodes that share the same parent node. For example, in `<ul><li>Item 1</li><li>Item 2</li></ul>`, the two `<li>` nodes are sibling nodes.

#### 10. **Document Object**

The `document` object is the main entry point for accessing the DOM. It provides methods and properties for retrieving and manipulating elements in the document. For example, `document.getElementById('myId')` returns an element with the specified ID.

#### 11. **DocumentFragment**

A `DocumentFragment` is a special object that represents a fragment of a document. It is a lightweight container for a portion of documents and can be used to build and modify portions of the DOM in memory before inserting them into the actual document. Using `DocumentFragment` can improve performance for DOM manipulations.

**Example:**

```javascript
var fragment = document.createDocumentFragment();

var newElement = document.createElement('div');

newElement.textContent = 'Element in the fragment';

fragment.appendChild(newElement);

document.body.appendChild(fragment);
```

#### 12. **Element Interface**

The `Element` interface represents an HTML or XML element in the DOM and provides methods and properties for accessing and modifying the element and its attributes. Some methods of the `Element` interface include `getAttribute()`, `setAttribute()`, `removeAttribute()`, and `querySelector()`.

**Example:**

```javascript
var element = document.getElementById('example');
element.setAttribute('class', 'newClass');
```

#### 13. **Node Interface**

The `Node` interface is the base for all interfaces representing nodes in the DOM. It provides general methods and properties for all node types, such as `nodeType`, `nodeName`, `childNodes`, and `parentNode`.

**Example:**

```javascript
var node =
```

```
document.getElementById('example');
console.log(node.nodeType); // Output: 1 for an element node
```

#### 14. **innerHTML**

The `innerHTML` property allows you to read or set the HTML content of an element. When you set `innerHTML`, the content of the element is replaced with the new HTML string.

**Example:**

```javascript
var element = document.getElementById('example');
element.innerHTML = '<p>New HTML content</p>';
```

```

#### 15. **textContent**

The `textContent` property allows you to read or set the text content of a node. Unlike `innerHTML`, `textContent` does not interpret the content as HTML.

**Example:**

```javascript
var element = document.getElementById('example');
element.textContent = 'Plain text without HTML';
```

#### 16. **createElement**
```

The `createElement(tagName)` method creates a new element with the specified tag name and returns it. This element can then be added to the DOM using methods like `appendChild()`.

**Example:**

```javascript
var newDiv = document.createElement('div');
newDiv.textContent = 'A new div element';
document.body.appendChild(newDiv);
```

#### 17. **appendChild**

The `appendChild(childNode)` method adds a child node to the end of the list of child nodes of a node. If the node is already in the DOM, it is removed from its original position and added to the new position.

**Example:**

```javascript
var element = document.createElement('p');
element.textContent = 'New paragraph';
document.body.appendChild(element);
```

#### 18. **removeChild**

The `removeChild(childNode)` method removes a specified child node from its parent node.

**Example:**

```javascript
var element =
```

```
document.getElementById('example');
element.parentNode.removeChild(element);
```

#### 19. **replaceChild**

The `replaceChild(newChild, oldChild)` method replaces an existing child node with a new child node.

**Example:**

```javascript
var newElement = document.createElement('p');
newElement.textContent = 'New content';
var oldElement = document.getElementById('oldElement');
oldElement.parentNode.replaceChild(newElement, oldElement);
```

```

#### 20. **cloneNode**

The `cloneNode(deep)` method creates a copy of a node. If `deep` is `true`, the node and all its descendants are copied. If `deep` is `false`, only the node itself is copied.

**Example:**

```javascript
var original = document.getElementById('example');
var copy = original.cloneNode(true);
document.body.appendChild(copy);
```

#### 21. **querySelector**
```

The `querySelector(selector)` method returns the first element that matches the specified CSS selector.

**Example:**

```javascript
var firstElement = document.querySelector('.class');
console.log(firstElement.textContent);
```

#### 22. **querySelectorAll**

The `querySelectorAll(selector)` method returns a NodeList of all elements that match the specified CSS selector.

**Example:**

```javascript
var allElements = document.querySelectorAll('.class');
allElements.forEach(function(element) {
    console.log(element.textContent);
});
```

#### 23. **addEventListener**

The `addEventListener(type, listener)` method adds an event listener to an element. Events can include clicks, inputs, and many others.

**Example:**

```javascript
var button =
```

```
document.getElementById('button');
button.addEventListener('click', function() {
    alert('Button clicked!');
});
```

#### 24. **removeEventListener**

The `removeEventListener(type, listener)` method removes an event listener that was previously added with `addEventListener`.

**Example:**

```javascript
var button = document.getElementById('button');
function handleClick() {
    alert('Button clicked!');
```

}

```
button.addEventListener('click', handleClick);
button.removeEventListener('click', handleClick);
```

#### 25. **event**

The `event` object represents an event that occurs in the DOM. It can include information such as the event type, the target element, and mouse coordinates.

**Example:**

```javascript
document.addEventListener('click', function(event) {
    console.log('Element clicked:', event.target);
```

});
```

####

26. **preventDefault**

The `preventDefault()` method prevents the default action associated with an event. For example, calling `preventDefault()` on a form submission event will prevent the form from submitting.

**Example:**

```javascript
document.getElementById('form').addEventListener('submit', function(event) {
    event.preventDefault();
    console.log('Form submission prevented');
```
```

});
```

#### 27. **stopPropagation**

The `stopPropagation()` method stops the event from propagating (bubbling) up or down the DOM hierarchy.

**Example:**

```javascript
document.getElementById('button').addEventListener('click', function(event) {
    event.stopPropagation();
    console.log('Event propagation stopped');
});
```
```

Understanding these DOM terms and concepts is essential for effective manipulation and interaction with web documents. Whether you're adding, removing, or modifying elements, or handling events, having a solid grasp of the DOM glossary will enhance your ability to work with the web's underlying structure and dynamics.

Here is the translation into English:

#### 28. **clientWidth and clientHeight**

The `clientWidth` and `clientHeight` properties return the inner width and height of an element, excluding borders and scrollbars.

**Example:**

```javascript
```

```javascript
var element = document.getElementById('example');

console.log('Client width:', element.clientWidth);

console.log('Client height:', element.clientHeight);
```

#### 29. **scrollWidth and scrollHeight**

The `scrollWidth` and `scrollHeight` properties return the total width and height of an element's content, including content not visible without scrolling.

**Example:**

```javascript
var element = document.getElementById('example');
```

```
console.log('Scroll width:', element.scrollWidth);

console.log('Scroll height:', element.scrollHeight);
```

#### 30. **style**

The `style` property represents the inline CSS applied to an element. It allows you to read and modify CSS property values directly through JavaScript.

**Example:**

```javascript
var element = document.getElementById('example');

element.style.color = 'red';

element.style.fontSize = '20px';
```

```

#### 31. **classList**

The `classList` property provides methods to manipulate the CSS classes of an element. It includes methods such as `add()`, `remove()`, `toggle()`, and `contains()`.

**Example:**

```javascript
var element = document.getElementById('example');
element.classList.add('newClass');
element.classList.remove('oldClass');
```

#### 32. **childNodes**
```

The `childNodes` property returns a NodeList of all child nodes of an element, including elements, text, and comments.

**Example:**

```javascript
var element = document.getElementById('example');
element.childNodes.forEach(function(node) {
    console.log(node.nodeType);
});
```

#### 33. **firstChild and lastChild**

The `firstChild` and `lastChild` properties return the first and last child nodes of an element.

**Example:**

```javascript
var element = document.getElementById('example');
console.log('First child:', element.firstChild);
console.log('Last child:', element.lastChild);
```

#### 34. **nextSibling and previousSibling**

The `nextSibling` and `previousSibling` properties return the node immediately following or preceding the current node, respectively, in the list of sibling nodes.

**Example:**

```javascript
var element = document.getElementById('example');

console.log('Next sibling:', element.nextSibling);

console.log('Previous sibling:', element.previousSibling);
```

#### 35. **nodeType**

The `nodeType` property returns a number representing the type of node. Common values include `1` for an element node, `3` for a text node, and `8` for a comment node.

**Example:**

```javascript
var element =
```

document.getElementById('example');
console.log('Node type:', element.nodeType);
```

#### 36. **nodeName**

The `nodeName` property returns the name of the node. For element nodes, it returns the tag name (e.g., `"DIV"` for a `<div>` element).

**Example:**

```javascript
var element = document.getElementById('example');
console.log('Node name:', element.nodeName);
```
```

#### 37. **nodeValue**

The `nodeValue` property returns or sets the value of a node. For text nodes, it returns the text contained in the node. For element nodes, it returns `null`.

**Example:**

```javascript
var textNode = document.createTextNode('Example text');
console.log('Node value:', textNode.nodeValue);
```

#### 38. **innerHTML vs outerHTML**

`innerHTML` returns or sets the HTML content of an element, while `outerHTML` returns or sets the entire HTML of an element, including the opening and closing tags.

**Example:**

```javascript
var element = document.getElementById('example');

console.log('innerHTML:', element.innerHTML);

console.log('outerHTML:', element.outerHTML);
```

#### 39. **setAttribute and getAttribute**

`setAttribute(name, value)` sets the value of a specified attribute on an element, while `getAttribute(name)` returns the value of an attribute.

**Example:**

```javascript
var element = document.getElementById('example');
element.setAttribute('data-info', 'some data');
console.log('Value of data-info attribute:', element.getAttribute('data-info'));
```

#### 40. **hasAttribute**

The `hasAttribute(name)` method checks if an element has a specified attribute.

**Example:**

```javascript
```

```javascript
var element = document.getElementById('example');
console.log('Has data-info attribute:', element.hasAttribute('data-info'));
```

#### 41. **removeAttribute**

The `removeAttribute(name)` method removes a specified attribute from an element.

**Example:**

```javascript
var element = document.getElementById('example');
element.removeAttribute('data-info');
```

#### 42. **className**

The `className` property returns or sets the value of an element's `class` attribute. Unlike `classList`, `className` handles classes as a single string.

**Example:**

```javascript
var element = document.getElementById('example');
element.className = 'newClass';
```

#### 43. **replaceWith**

The `replaceWith(newNode)` method replaces the current node with a new node.

**Example:**

```javascript
var element = document.getElementById('example');
var newElement = document.createElement('p');
newElement.textContent = 'Replaced element';
element.replaceWith(newElement);
```

#### 44. **insertAdjacentHTML**

The `insertAdjacentHTML(position, text)` method inserts the specified HTML text into a position relative to the element.

**Example:**

```javascript
var element = document.getElementById('example');

element.insertAdjacentHTML('beforeend', '<p>New paragraph added.</p>');
```

#### 45. **createDocumentFragment**

The `createDocumentFragment()` method creates a document fragment, which is a lightweight node structure used to collect and manipulate a portion of the DOM.

**Example:**

```javascript
var fragment = document.createDocumentFragment();

var div = document.createElement('div');
```

```
div.textContent = 'Content in the fragment';
fragment.appendChild(div);
document.body.appendChild(fragment);
```

#### 46. **getElementsByTagName**

The `getElementsByTagName(tagName)` method returns a NodeList of all elements with the specified tag name.

**Example:**

```javascript
var paragraphs = document.getElementsByTagName('p');
for (var i = 0; i < paragraphs.length; i++) {
    console.log(paragraphs[i].textContent);
}
```

```

#### 47. **getElementsByClassName**

The `getElementsByClassName(className)` method returns an HTMLCollection of all elements with the specified class.

**Example:**

```javascript
var elements = document.getElementsByClassName('class');
for (var i = 0; i < elements.length; i++) {
    console.log(elements[i].textContent);
}
```

#### 48. **getElementById**
```

The `getElementById(id)` method returns the element with the specified ID.

**Example:**

```javascript
var element = document.getElementById('example');
console.log(element.textContent);
```

#### 49. **createTextNode**

The `createTextNode(data)` method creates a text node with the specified data.

**Example:**

```javascript
var text = document.createTextNode('Example text');
document.body.appendChild(text);
```

#### 50. **createTextNode**

The `createTextNode(data)` method creates a text node with the specified data. This text node can be inserted into a DOM element to display the text within the element.

**Example:**

```javascript
var text = document.createTextNode('Example text');
var paragraph = document.createElement('p');
paragraph.appendChild(text);
```

```
document.body.appendChild(paragraph);
```

In this example, a text node is created with the content 'Example text'. Then, a `<p>` element is created, and the text node is added as a child of this element. Finally, the `<p>` element is added to the document body.

#### 51. **importNode**

The `importNode(node, deep)` method imports a node from one document to another. The `deep` parameter specifies whether to include descendant nodes.

**Example:**

```javascript
var originalNode = document.getElementById('example');
```

```
var newDocument = document.implementation.createHTMLDocument();

var importedNode = newDocument.importNode(originalNode, true);

newDocument.body.appendChild(importedNode);
```

This example shows how to import a node from the current document into a new HTML document. The `true` option for the `deep` parameter indicates that all descendant nodes should be imported.

# Index

**1. Introduction pg.4**

**2. Introduction of DOM pg.28**

**3. DOM Approaches and Techniques pg.38**

**4. The DOM in Browsers pg.61**

**5. Examples and Applications of the DOM pg.79**

**6. DOM Glossary: Definitions and Key Concepts pg.100**

www.ingramcontent.com/pod-product-compliance
Lightning Source LLC
Chambersburg PA
CBHW050259230526
45471CB00005B/1951